BORN
TO
NEW LIFE

Cyprian of Carthage

The Spirituality of the Fathers

2

BORN
TO
NEW LIFE

Cyprian of Carthage

edited by
Oliver Davies

translated by
Tim Witherow

introduction by
Cyprian Smith, O.S.B.

New City Press
New Rochelle, New York

Published in the United States by New City Press
86 Mayflower Avenue, New Rochelle, New York 10801
©1992 New City, London, Great Britain

Translations by Tim Witherow

Library of Congress Cataloging-in-Publication Data:

Cyprian, Saint, Bishop of Carthage.
  [Selections. English. 1992]
  Born to new life / Cyprian of Carthage ; edited by Oliver
Davies ; translated by Tim Witherow ; introduction by
Cyprian Smith.

  Includes bibliographical references.
  ISBN 1-56548-006-6 : $7.95
  1. Christian life—Early church, ca. 30-600. 2. Cyprian, Saint,
Bishop of Carthage. 3. Church history–Primitive and early
church, ca. 30-600–Sources. 4. Carthage (Extinct city)–Church
history. I. Davies, Oliver. II. Title.
BR65.C82E539 1992
270.1—dc20   92-14860

Printed in the United States of America

Contents

Selected Letters 117

Short Bibliography 127

Introduction

Can the writings of a third century bishop of Carthage have much value for Christians living in the very different world of the late twentieth century? At first glance we might not think so. On closer examination, however, some very real points of contact emerge into view. Our world, like his, is marked by violence, restlessness, insecurity and injustice. Thoughtful and sensitive people in our day, as in his, tend to react to this situation in two ways. On the one hand, they develop a great interest in the inner life of the spirit: hence the revival of interest in mysticism; the popularity of retreat centers; the rising flood of literature on prayer and meditation. On the other, they develop an intense concern for social justice and concrete, practical aid to the poor and oppressed. The modern Church has advanced quite dramatically on both these fronts, though the question of how to balance and integrate them remains an awkward one. It may be that in our day, as in Cyprian's, such integration can come about only through martyrdom in some shape or form: either the public martyrdom whereby we bear witness to our innermost convictions in the face of persecution by a hostile society; or the more secret, private martyrdom whereby we wage inward battle against the worldliness and selfishness which our weak nature and secular culture invite us to every day and every hour.

If we look to Cyprian's writings for inspiration and guidance on these matters, we shall not be disappointed, since he has much to say on all of them. We cannot accuse him, for example, of ignorance concerning the inner life of the spirit. The great modern psychologist, C. G. Jung, complained that many modern Christians are too "externalized" in their religious outlook; that the redemption offered by Christ is not a reality in their inner lives, which remain, in fact, unrepentantly pagan; that the Church offers them symbols, but not the reality, of transformation. The treatise *To Donatus,* however, makes it clear that Cyprian's view is quite different. The power of the spirit, flowing from baptism and the other sacraments of the Church, together with the illumination and purification which come from frequent pondering of the Word of God, can effect a real transformation, a real birth to new life. Not that such a transformation can be brought about once and for all, so that we can then sit back and take things easy. Cyprian emphasizes that growth in the Spirit is an ongoing process, which never reaches its conclusion in this life, but only in the next. It cannot happen unless we are always ready for new insights, new acts of generosity and surrender, whereby we let go of our former selfish drives and allow ourselves to be moved and directed by the Spirit.

It is quite clear, too, that Cyprian has a thirst for justice and altruism in social relationships which makes him quite the equal of any modern reformer. In the treatise *To Donatus* his scalding denunciation of contemporary social evils shows how strong was his moral revulsion when faced with the corruption and hypocrisy of life under the late Roman Empire, and it is not hard for the reader to find modern equivalents for the various monstrosities. Yet neither is it possible for Cyprian, any more than for modern Christians, merely to turn their backs upon a hopelessly corrupt world and concentrate on their own individual salvation. We have a duty to combat social injustice by giving material aid to the poor and underprivileged; the treatise *On Works and Alms* is one of the longest and most eloquent of Cyprian's writings and it shows how deep was his feeling in this matter. He also regards it as the inescapable duty of the Christian to bear public witness to the faith, even though this could mean imprisonment, torture and death; and here Cyprian is a co-witness with the suffering Church in many parts of the world today.

There is no need to harp any further on this theme. Readers of Cyprian's writings will not find it difficult to discover further areas where his preoccupations are similar to our own. If we see him exclusively from this standpoint, however, our reading of him is likely to remain somewhat superficial and ultimately unfruitful. There is little point in our reading the great writers of the past in order to confirm our own ideas (or prejudices). One of the greatest services a figure from the remote past can render us is to provide us with a viewpoint that is *different* from our own, in some ways perhaps even diametrically opposed to our own, precisely because it emanates from a different mentality and culture. So as we read the various short works of Cyprian included in the present volume, it is perhaps worth asking ourselves the question: is there some aspect of human and Christian life which he understands more clearly than we do, or which at any rate he views in a different way? Opinions may differ about this; but if there is any characteristic feature of Cyprian's outlook which is vitally important for our proper understanding of him, but which we may fail to appreciate because of our very different culture and historical conditions, it is perhaps his *unworldliness.*

It has never been part of the Church's teaching, either official or unofficial, to maintain that we can find total or final fulfillment of our human and spiritual aspirations in this world, or in the present life. Christian teaching has always had that which is called "eschatological," which sees the present time as something provisional and preparatory to something greater, whether this greater fulfillment is seen as lying beyond the grave or at some mysterious point in the future in which all our deepest hopes and aspirations can find total fulfillment. Our life here is a journey, and our goal is out of sight, over the horizon; it is a battle, and the final outcome is not yet settled. Eschatology is one thing; utopianism is quite another, and it is only the former that is truly Christian.

This sense of the provisional and temporary character of the world we live in, this looking beyond to a world not conditioned by space, time and change, is not a dominant note in all Christian thinking or speaking in the modern age. We have a tendency to stress the goodness and value of human life in the present world *just as it is.* Such an attitude would have appeared strange to Cyprian and by no means entirely acceptable. Whether we will it or not, we are all influenced to a great extent by the attitudes of secular humanism, which condition our thoughts in a way that they could not do with his. If we strive, for example, to give aid to the poor and oppressed, to combat unjust social and political structures, to relieve the sufferings of humanity, this is surely in part because we believe that human beings have certain rights, that they possess an innate dignity, and that the present world can be made substantially better than it is. Perhaps Cyprian would have agreed with all this—up to a point. But he would not have liked the stress we lay upon this aspect of the question. The latent utopianism behind much of this thinking would have been especially repugnant to him. It is true, of course, that from Plato onwards sensitive and thoughtful people have diverted themselves by imagining an ideal political state with ideal institutions. To attempt to realize such fantasies in actual political reality, however, is a comparatively modern phenomenon, scarcely three centuries old. The fallacy of this approach is that it not only imagines ideal institutions for humanity, but also an ideal humanity for the institutions. Whether either of these can ever be realized in fact is open to question. Traditional Christian faith would seem to suggest that they cannot.

Cyprian certainly thought that they could not. For him our true home is not here but elsewhere, beyond the grave or in a New Age, brought about not by human efforts and progress, but by an explosion of the previously restrained power of God. This conviction colors his outlook and makes it very different from ours, even when he is speaking of matters which preoccupy us as much as they do him. He is horrified at the corruption and injustice proliferating in the late Roman Empire, but this does not lead him to rebel against the emperor, to attempt to change the social structures which foster these horrors. Why? Because he sees the present world and its institutions as essentially provisional and imperfect, and there are very definite limits to the improvement we can hope to bring about in this area, because this world is not the place where we are ultimately meant to be; it is not our final home. It is in part, a very large part, under the sway of sin and the powers of darkness. Our task is not so much to change it, as to battle against it, to confront it, and by our faith and steadfastness in the power of God, fit ourselves for a higher spiritual world, the kingdom of heaven, over which evil and corruption have no hold. Thus the martyrdom sought by Cyprian and his followers is subtly different from the death voluntarily incurred by a modern freedom-fighter or prisoner of conscience. Cyprian was not hoping, through the nonviolent resistance of martyrdom, to bring the Roman Empire to its knees, as Gandhi hoped to do with the British Empire. His eyes were not on this world but on the next, and martyrdom was his passport to this last. The same conviction underlies his attitude to almsgiving and works of mercy; he stresses their importance and necessity, but not primarily in order to improve the common lot of humanity, which would be our primary aim today. The value of almsgiving for him lies principally in the fact that it *purifies us from sin,* that is, it enables us to escape from this present world into a far better one.

How are we to react, once we realize this fundamental difference between Cyprian's outlook and our own? Shall we turn away from him in despair, concluding that he has nothing to say to us today? That would be a great mistake. It would be tantamount to rejecting him simply because he does not passively reflect our own views, does not confirm us in our own preconceived ideas. Perhaps his different perspective does not simply contradict our own, but, properly understood, can combine with it, enrich it and complement it. Once we consider this possibility, then two truths emerge.

The first is that Cyprian's "other-worldliness" does not make him cold, inhuman, or inaccessible. He is perfectly capable of appreciating and enjoying the ordinary pleasures of life, such as a quiet meal in the company of a good friend in attractive scenery—so much is clear from the treatise *To Donatus.* He is no Puritan regarding pleasure as intrinsically sinful. Neither is his compassion for the poor motivated by a merely selfish concern for his own salvation; a good deal of human warmth and sympathy is perceptible in his treatise *On Works and Alms.* What

12

he says about the power of the Spirit to effect a real transformation in a person's life is not based on mere theorizing; it is the fruit of his own intensely lived personal experience. Perhaps it is in his treatises *On Patience* and *On the Death Rate* that he appears most attractive and sympathetic, for in these works, in which he grapples with the problem of pain and suffering in the world, he is no detached observer, but one who lives and suffers together with those whom he is trying to help. If he is able to look "beyond" our present human world, that is not because he is not really in it, or because he does not know it from the inside. None of his writings is merely theoretical; they all spring from a response to real-life situations.

Lastly, if he is more intent upon the other world, upon the transcendent, than it is altogether easy for us to be, is he at fault in this? As Christians we all live on the razor-edge of paradox, striving to be in the world but not of it, to live in time but also in eternity, to be aware of the seen but also of the unseen. Few of us manage to achieve a true balance between them. Perhaps Cyprian stressed the other world too much; but does not that make him an excellent antidote for our own malady, which is to stress the present world too much? Recognizing clearly this tension of opposites, this clash of contraries, which lies at the heart of our religion—and indeed of any attempt to view life wisely and realistically—perhaps we shall learn to see ourselves and our world as they really are, and thus prepare ourselves for the ultimate revelation of the Absolute Truth which is the goal of all our striving. With these thoughts in mind, we can profitably turn to Cyprian's writings and ponder them well.

Cyprian Smith, O.S.B.

Life and Works of Cyprian of Carthage

The third century was a time of great trial for all Christians as cruel and destructive persecutions swept through the Roman Empire under Decius, Valerius and Diocletian. Decius (249-51) demanded that all citizens should prove that they had offered sacrifice to the emperor, or face the death penalty. In the event, many were killed, and many fell from the faith (becoming known as the *lapsi*).

But during this time of trial, the Church found a great champion in Cyprian (Caeculius Cyprianus Thascius), who had been born of wealthy parents between 200 and 210, was converted to Christianity around the year 246, was ordained shortly afterwards, and became Bishop of Carthage in the year 248 or 249. Cyprian led the African Church during these turbulent and violent times, and thus he became involved in two major controversies which arose out of the persecution.

The first of these was the proper attitude of the "confessing" Church to those of its members who had lapsed under the threat of punishment. In his treatise *On the Lapsed* Cyprian advocated a middle course, treating the sin as a grave one but not irreparable. He thus made it possible for the lapsed to return to the Church after a suitable period of penance. The schismatics however, who were a powerful influence in Northern Africa and who found a leader in the person of Novatian, took a more extreme view and they denied that it was possible to receive lapsed Christians back into the Church at all.

These uncompromising and severe schismatics were themselves a threat to Cyprian and to the Catholic

Church, and when schismatics sought to return to the Catholic Church, the bishop demanded that they should be rebaptized. Following the custom of the Church in Africa, Cyprian denied the validity of their sacraments. This clashed however with the position of Pope Stephen, the Bishop of Rome. Cyprian maintained that sacraments could not be validly administered outside the true Church of Christ, while Pope Stephen argued that the sacraments were valid, as long as they were properly administered, even if the ministers were themselves heretics or schismatics. As a result of this conflict Cyprian wrote *On the Unity of the Church,* which is a document of great historical value. In it the Bishop sets out the nature of the one true Church (in a third century context), which is founded upon the See of Rome and is expressed in the episcopate. In a second version of the treatise, also by Cyprian himself, the role of the papacy is played down. This document is thus the very first theological discussion which we possess on the authority of the pope or the local bishop to decide concerning matters of practice and principle; and here Cyprian's two versions show his ambivalence. The debate was cut short, however, when Stephen was martyred in 256 and, two years later, Cyprian himself was beheaded outside Carthage.

Rather than works of purely historical or doctrinal interest, this anthology contains pieces in which we see something of Cyprian the Christian, and in which he addresses the universal concerns of Christian living. The treatise *To Donatus,* for instance, was written in 246 or 247, shortly after Cyprian's conversion, and in it he speaks with great force of the deep change within his life. *On the Death Rate* was written in 252 or 253 during the plague which struck Carthage after the end of the

Decian persecution. In this work Cyprian addresses with great wisdom the reality of physical suffering and death from the perspective of the Christian faith. The plague left much poverty in its wake, and *On Works and Alms,* which dates from 253, is an appeal to the Christian community to give generously to the poor and to care for those who are in distress. *On the Benefit of Patience,* written in 256, shows Cyprian's deep understanding of suffering and his belief in the positive use which the Christian can make of times of difficulty. Patience, for Cyprian, is a divine attribute, and in practicing it we become like God. Finally, there is a small selection from Cyprian's letters, which number eighty-one in all (including sixteen that were written to him). Of the letters which appear here, one was written to those Christians who were awaiting their martyrdom in prison. This is a moving letter (number thirty-seven) of great power and beauty. Extracts from a second letter (number sixty-three) show Cyprian's understanding of the eucharist, and a last letter, the final one of the corpus (number eighty-one) was written just before Cyprian himself returned to Carthage in order to meet his own death for Christ.

Oliver Davies

To Donatus

Sharing Personal Experience

My dear Donatus, you are quite right to remind me of the promise I made you, and which I had not forgotten. Now is a good time to keep it when the harvest feast offers us some free time, and our minds can relax and enjoy this regular respite during the labors of the year. The place too suits the season for the pleasant prospect of the gardens and the gentle breezes of autumn combine to soothe and calm the senses. In this setting we can spend the day in delightful conversation and instruct our hearts with the teachings of the Lord.

Let us find somewhere to sit where our discussion will not be inhibited by the presence of a stranger or disturbed by the excessive noise of family squabbles. Close by is a secluded spot for us to retire where vine shoots luxuriate in unrestrained clumps around the canes which support them and frame a portico of tendrils with a leafy roof. Here we will be able to delight our ears in study and, when we look around at the trees and vines, enrich our gaze at the wonderful sight. So at the same time as we instruct our heart with what is said, we can nourish our eyes with what we see. I know, however, that your sole care and concern will be with what we are saying. You will ignore the charms of the delightful scene around you, keeping your eyes firmly fixed on mine, and with your face and your mind, and because of the love you feel for me, you will be completely absorbed in listening.

But how much and what kinds of things can I teach you? Yet, though my poor intelligence can produce only a small and meager crop which hardly burdens the ground with its heavy harvest, I shall nevertheless bring forth as much as I can since the actual subject matter lends me support. For if you are speaking in court, before the assembly or the senate, a lavish and extravagant eloquence is appropriate. But before God, our master, the absolute sincerity of our speech is supported not by our arguments but rather by our actions. And so accept these words that have power rather than facility and are designed not to win over a popular audience by their fancy turns of phrase, but to preach the mercy of God by the naked simplicity of the truth. Accept that which has been sincerely felt rather than merely learned, that which has not been laboriously accumulated over the course of a long apprenticeship but seized in an instant by a sudden act of grace.

(1-2)

Born Again through Baptism

Once I lay in darkness and in the depths of night and was tossed to and fro in the waves of the turbulent world, uncertain of the correct way to go, ignorant of my true life and a stranger to the light of truth. At that time and on account of the life I then led, it seemed difficult to believe what divine mercy promised for my salvation, namely, that someone could be born again and to a new life by being immersed in the healing water of baptism. It was difficult to believe that though I would remain the same man in bodily form, my heart and mind would be transformed.

How was it possible, I thought, that a change could be great enough to strip away in a single moment the innate hardness of our nature? How could the habits acquired over the course of many years disappear, since these are so deeply rooted within us? If someone is used to fine feasts and lavish banquets, how can they learn restraint? If someone is used to dressing conspicuously in gold and purple, how can they cast them aside for ordinary simple clothes? Someone who loves the trappings of public office cannot become an anonymous private person. Anyone who is attended by great crowds of supporters and is honored by a dense entourage of obsequious attendants would consider solitude a punishment. While temptation still holds us fast, we are seduced by wine, inflated with pride, inflamed by anger, troubled by greed, goaded by cruelty, enticed by ambition and cast headlong by lust.

These were my frequent thoughts. For I was held fast by the many sins of my life from which it seemed impossible for me to extricate myself. Thus I yielded to my sins which clung fast to me. Since I despaired of improvement I took an indulgent view of my faults and regarded them as if they were slaves born in my house.

But after the life-giving water of baptism came to my rescue and washed away the stain of my former years and poured into my cleansed and purified heart the light which comes from above, and after I had drunk in the Heavenly Spirit and was made a new man by a second birth, then amazingly what I had previously doubted became clear to me. What had been hidden was revealed. What had been dark became light. What previously had seemed impossible now seemed possible. What was in me of the guilty flesh now confessed it was earthly. What was made alive in me by the Holy Spirit was now quickened by God.

(3-4)

Our Transformation is God's Gift

I am sure you will recognize as well as I did what I gained from the death of sin and the birth of virtue. You know that yourself, there is no need to tell you. It would be wrong to sing my own praises, since what was due to God's beneficence rather than an individual's virtue should be an occasion for gratitude rather than boasting. Absence of sin is a mark of faith just as before sin was a mark of human error.

From God, I say, everything we are capable of comes from God: from him we live, from him we grow and from him we take the strength with which we may understand in the present the signs of what is to come. May the guardian of our innocence be the fear which God in his heavenly mercy has shone into our hearts, and may it find a secure resting place in a heart which pleases him and may we not allow laziness to corrupt the security we have been given or allow the old enemy to steal back again.

(4)

Living the New Life

But if you want to follow the path of innocence and justice and walk with a firm and unfailing step, holding to God with all your heart and strength, you must be what this beginning has made you.

Your power to do this will be in accordance with the increase of spiritual grace. For, unlike the way in which gifts are given here on earth, there will be no limit to the kind and number of the gifts which God will bestow on us. The Spirit is poured forth with a generosity that knows no limits and is unconstrained by any barriers or definite limit. It flows in torrents without ceasing into our thirsting heart. We will drink as much grace as the faith which we bring. And it is this which enables us, with the morality of our life and the purity of our mind and voice, to extinguish the raging poison which burns the sick to the marrow, to cleanse the defilement of the foolish by bringing them back to health, to bring peace to the enemy, calm to the violent and gentleness to the wild.

Thus insofar as we are what we have begun to be, the Spirit we have received enjoys its state of freedom; but insofar as we have not changed our body and limbs, our sight is obscured by the cloud of this world. How powerful is the Spirit, what strength to be able to withdraw from the pernicious contact with the world, since someone who has been cleansed and purified cannot be defiled by contact with the enemy, but indeed is made so much stronger that they can exercise power and dominion over a whole army ranged against them!

(5)

The Darkness of the World

And so that the signs of this divine gift may shine more brightly in the clear light of the truth, I shall illuminate you by casting aside the cloud of evil and darkness that lies over the world. Imagine that you have been carried off to the summit of some high mountain and that you are looking down on what lies below. You move your eyes over the land you have been taken from and gaze on the troubles of the world. You will at once look on life with pity and, after considering your own position, you will congratulate yourself and feel a surge of joy because you have escaped all this.

Look down at the roads full of robbers, the sea infested with pirates and military bases spreading war and slaughter everywhere. It is a world wet with the blood of people slaughtering each other, where murder is regarded as a crime if committed by individuals but is called a public service when carried out *en masse,* as if it were not the question of innocence but the extent of the savagery that determines freedom from guilt.

Now turn your eyes and gaze toward the cities whose crowds you will find bleaker than any solitude. A gladiatorial show is on at which cruel people feast their eyes and satisfy their lust for blood. The body here is fed on nourishing food and its great muscled bulk is fattened merely so that its slaughter may present a more lavish sacrifice. Human beings are killed for the pleasure of human beings, and people are even trained in the art and practice of killing: crime is not only committed but taught.

Is there any sight more miserable? People are taught

to slaughter and find their fame in that activity. And what, I ask you, do you think of the fact that human beings in the prime of their lives, with beautiful bodies and lavish clothes, and without having been condemned to it, actually choose to fight wild beasts? While still alive they dress up for their own funerals and delight in their own misery and troubles. It is madness not punishment which drives them to fight wild animals. Fathers watch their own sons, sisters watch their own brothers and, if a more elaborate spectacle requires greater expenditure, then a mother will pay for it so that she may be present at her own grief. At such godless and vile spectacles, they forget that their eyes are at the very least an accomplice to murder.

If only from your high vantage point you could penetrate the most secret places, unbolt the doors of bedrooms and expose the most hidden recesses to the full glare of vision, you would see the shameless commit acts which would revolt a modest glance. You would see what is a crime even to look at; you would see what people, crazed by the fires of their lust, deny and yet rush headlong to commit. Deranged by desire they thrust themselves at each other. Acts are committed which even their perpetrators dislike.

It is true that criminals accuse those who are most like them, the base defame the base and think that their knowledge of what is done constitutes their innocence rather than their guilt. Thus the very people who publicly accuse others commit in secret the same offenses; the criminals act as censors. They condemn outside what they indulge inside, freely doing what they censor. Such audacity and impudence suits their shameful vice. Do not be surprised at what they say, for their words are the least of their crimes.

26

But now, after you have heard about the roads full of robbers, the many conflicts spread over the surface of the earth, the repulsive slaughter at the games, the disgusting debauchery offered by brothel keepers or done in the seclusion of the home, where its concealment makes daring greater, you may think that the forum is immune from open outrage and criminal actions. But just look there and you will find even more terrible things which will force you to avert your eyes.

Although the laws have been engraved on the twelve tablets and the statutes fixed in bronze for all to see, yet even in the shadow of the very laws and statutes wrong is committed and integrity not retained where it should above all be defended. The fury of competing lawyers rages and, where togas are worn, the peace is shattered and the forum resounds with mad litigation. Here you find the spear and sword and executioner, hooks to pierce and racks to stretch, fire to burn and more instruments to torture the human body than it has limbs. Who can come to a person's rescue? Their patron? But he prevaricates and deceives. The judge? But he sells his sentence. The judge whose task it is to punish criminal actions commits one himself when the innocent defendant is condemned to death.

Crime is rife everywhere, and the noxious poison multiplies the forms of crime working through shameless spirits. Wills are forged, fraudulent documents are drawn up, children are kept from their inheritance, people's property is given to complete strangers, the adversary accuses, the slanderer attacks and the witness commits perjury. On every side the shameless greed of advocates slides on in its work of false accusation; while the guilty escape the ruin of the innocent. The laws inspire no fear, nor does the judge, and what is no longer

27

binding is no longer feared. Those who are guilty regard innocence as a crime, and anyone who does not imitate them offends them. The law has become a party to crime and made it legal by doing it in public. What sense of shame and decency can remain intact when there is no one to condemn evil people except those who ought themselves to be condemned?

(6, 7, 9, 10)

Popular Delusions

Perhaps I seem to have selected only examples of bad things and, in my enthusiasm to condemn, have directed you to the sad and unpleasant side of life which would outrage any decent conscience. Let me now point out to you those things that our age, in all its ignorance, regards as worth having.

For even what I am about to show you should be avoided. Those things that you are accustomed to regard as marks of honor, the emblems of power, wealth and affluence, influence in the army, the purple robes of public office, authority to rule as you desire, all these are only the hidden poison of evils which tempt you. They are the smiling face of sin and the enticing deception of treacherous attraction. They are like the poison whose deadly juices have been masked by a sprinkling of sugar and doctored to seem like an ordinary drink but, once swallowed, its fatal power takes effect.

When you see a man in conspicuous dress and fairly gleaming, or so he thinks, in purple, just consider the dirty tricks that got him to this splendor. Consider the sort of arrogant rebuffs he had to suffer, how he sat out on the door-steps of pompous men to perform the early morning greeting, how many times he wedged himself into the seething crowds of clients and how often he went on procession so that he too could one day have his own crowd of supporters to accompany him as a tribute not to his individual worth but to his power. Indeed, he is respected not for his character but for his influence. Just imagine how his wretched entourage will depart, his time-serving flatterers leave him when he becomes an ordinary man and is abandoned to dishonor. Then they will realize the harm that has been done to their assets, notice that their estate is now worth nothing, and see the financial cost of their pursuit of the fickle breezes of the public whim and all vain and earthly promises. The whole business is as a waste of time, a gigantic public circus in which the people remain dissatisfied and the candidate is lost.

And as for those you regard as wealthy, who constantly increase their land and throw the poor out beyond the boundary marks and so extend their estates without limits, those who possess great treasuries of wealth in gold and silver heaped up or buried, even people such as these find that their peace of mind is disturbed. They are filled with fear and anxiety that robbers or assassins will attack them or that they will attract the unwelcome attentions of even richer men who will try and defraud them. They can neither eat nor sleep in peace. At the banquet they sigh, while they drink from gem-encrusted goblets. And although they fall exhausted into a deep and yielding couch, the soft down allows them no repose.

The wretched person fails to realize that these are torments in disguise. They do not see that they are held captive by their gold, that they are the slave rather than the master of their wealth, and—what hateful blindness of mind and profound darkness of greed!—when they could unload and unburden themselves of their encumbrances, they just brood even more on the wealth that tortures them and cling more tightly still to the punishments they have amassed for themselves. They refuse to give money to their clients, or share it with the poor, and while they call their money their own, they shut it away at home and vigilantly guard it as if it belonged to someone else. They do not even share any of it with their friends, their children or even with themselves. They can only be said to possess it inasmuch as they stop anyone else from possessing it, and—what strange perversion of names!—they call "goods" what they use purely for bad ends.

Do you really think that those who live among the symbols of honor and whose great wealth appears to have deep foundations are really safe in the gleaming splendor of their royal palaces and armed guards? They feel more rather than less anxiety since fear is in proportion to the grounds for it. This very power exacts an equally great penalty from those who are even more powerful, even though they try to protect themselves with a dense guard of security men. They are unable to enjoy that freedom of mind which they make sure their inferiors are also deprived of. The rich are terrified of the power which they use to terrify others: it grins so that it may deceive, it raises up so it may cast down. Power exacts a progressive rate of interest: the larger the amount of prestige, the more punitive is the interest on it.

(11-13)

31

The Sure Source of Peace

The only truly secure and reliable source of peace, the one solid and firm basis for security is to take yourself away from the tempests of this troubling world and find calm in the port of salvation. And thus to be able to lift up your eyes from the earth to heaven and bring your mind close to God, and there take joy in the fact that whatever seems great and important here on earth falls short of the feeling within your heart.

Once we are raised above our age, we can seek and desire nothing from it. How firm and unshakable is that protection, how divine the guardianship in its never ending bestowal of riches, which releases you from the snares of the world, purges you from the cesspit of earth and brings you into the light of eternity. You will see the creeping and insidious danger, which previously threatened us, for what it really is. We shall be impelled to love more what we are to become, the more we confess and condemn what we once were.

In this task we have no need to spend money or engage in frantic campaigning as if we had to win the respect and protection of some powerful man by our diligence. It is a gift of God freely given. The Heavenly Spirit is given as spontaneously as the sun shines, the day is bright, the stream flows or the rain falls. When the heart has looked to heaven and recognized its true master, it becomes higher than the sun, more powerful than anything on earth and it begins to be what it believes itself to be.

(14)

Live in God

You who have set up camp in the spiritual realm of heaven, preserve your integrity and your sobriety and exercise the discipline of spiritual virtues.

Speak and study without cease. Speak with God and allow God to speak with you. Let his teaching instruct and inform your life. Whoever God has enriched nobody shall impoverish. Poverty cannot touch anyone whose heart is nourished by divine food. Ceilings guilded with fine gold and mansions full of precious marble slabs will seem of no value to you when you know that it is your soul that should be protected and refined and that a house in which the Lord sits as in a temple and in which the Holy Spirit has begun to dwell is the best possible house of all.

Let us paint this house with the colors of innocence, and light it with justice. Never will it collapse with the passage of time, nor will the walls lose their sheen of gold and paint. Pretty things have only a short life-span and provide their owners with a false permanence since they are not possessed in any true sense. But what is truly possessed remains brilliantly clothed and, untarnished, shines out forever. It cannot be destroyed or extinguished but only formed to an ever greater perfection.

This will be enough for the time being, my dear Donatus, for even though an easy and loving disposition, and a mind constant in its faith takes delight in listening to good conversation, and I know that nothing pleases your ears as much as that which will please God, we ought nevertheless to bring our conversation to an end. We live close to each other and can easily speak again.

And since the holiday offers us both peace and time for leisure, let us enjoy what remains of the day as the sun begins to set toward evening and fill the time of our eating with the grace of heaven.

Let us enjoy a psalm as we begin our modest meal. And since your memory is so good and your voice even better, you can perform that task, as you usually do. For we will enjoy our meal much more if it is accompanied by some spiritual music to soothe our ears.

(15-16)

On the Benefit of Patience

The Value of Patience

My dear brothers and sisters, since the subject I am preparing to speak to you about is patience, setting forth its benefits and advantages, what better place is there for me to begin than by saying that I feel your patience is necessary in listening to me now, since your patience will most certainly be required as you listen to what I am about to say.

For it is only when patience is present that lessons and lectures can be taken in with profit. And indeed, my dear brothers and sisters, I have never found anything of greater importance for learning how to live a better life or for increasing our glory among all the various paths of divine teaching, than that we should hold closely to the commandments of the Lord, in the obedience that comes from fear and devotion, and in particular, that we should be alert to the need for patience as much as we possibly can.

(1)

True Patience is Rooted in God

The Stoic philosophers do indeed profess to follow this, but in their case their patience is as false as the rest of their wisdom. For how can anyone claim to know what patience is without being familiar with the patience of God?

He himself gives a warning to those who think that they are wise in this world and says: "I will destroy the wisdom of the wise, and will bring to nothing the understanding of the prudent." Similarly, the blessed Paul, who was filled with the Holy Spirit when he had been sent out to preach to the Gentiles, bears witness and says in his teaching: "Take care that you are not perverted by philosophy and that vain science which seeks to understand the elements of this world and fails to see Christ where the site of true divinity is." And in another place: "Let no one deceive himself; if anyone among you believes that he is wise then let him become a fool in this world so that he may become wise. For it is written: 'The Lord condemns those in their wisdom,' and again: 'The Lord knows that the thoughts of the wise are foolish.'"

And so if true wisdom is not with them neither can true patience be. For if the mark of a patient person is humility and mildness, and if we find that philosophers are far from being either humble or mild but are in fact conceited and, being so pleased with themselves, they cannot please God, then it is clear that true patience must be absent where the arrogant seeds of their free-thinking are present.

But let us, my dear brothers and sisters, who are not philosophers only in our speech but in our actions, who do not claim to be wise by wearing a certain style of dress but in truth, who do not merely boast about virtues but have firsthand experience of them, and who do not talk about noble things but actually live out our life according to our doctrines, let us, as servants and worshippers of God, show that patience which comes from spiritual submission and which we have learned from the teachings of heaven. For we hold this virtue in common with God. Patience begins with him; he is the source of its radiance and dignity. The origin and greatness of patience comes from God its author. We ought to love whatever is dear to God. The majesty of God commends the good it loves. If God is our Lord and Father, then let us follow the patience of him who is both Lord and Father to us, for it is the duty of servants to obey, and it is wrong for children to show resistance.

(2-3)

Patience is an Aspect of Love

And so that we might be able, my dear brothers and sisters, to understand that patience is a thing of God, and that whoever is kind and patient and mild is like God our Father, the Lord gave us instructions for salvation in his gospel and pronounced divine warnings so that his disciples might become perfect, and said: "You have heard it said that you should love your neighbor and hate your enemy, but I say to you that you should love your enemies and pray for those who persecute you, so that you may be the children of your Father who is in heaven and who makes his sun rise on the good and on the evil, and lets the rain fall on the just and on the unjust alike. For if you love those who love you, what reward shall you have when even the publicans do that? So be more perfect, just as your Father in heaven is perfect."

He told us that we will become perfect sons and daughters of God, and taught us that we will be made whole after being reformed by a heavenly birth, if the patience of God our Father dwells in us, and if the divine likeness which Adam lost by his sin becomes clear and shines forth in what we do. What glory it would be to become like God, how great a joy it would be to exhibit those virtues which can be worthy of divine praise!

(5)

Jesus, the Model of Patience

And moreover, my dear brothers and sisters, Jesus Christ our God and master did not just teach us this by his words, but fulfilled it in his own actions. And since he said that he had come down to earth to do the will of his Father, among the other wonderful virtues he possessed as proof of his divine majesty, he preserved the patience of his Father by the strength of his tolerance.

All his actions from the very moment of his arrival here on earth are singled out by the presence of his patience. For by first coming down to earth from heaven above, he showed that he did not disdain to put on human flesh, and while he himself was not a sinner, he did not disdain to bear the sins of others. Thus in casting off his immortality and allowing himself to be made mortal, he allowed himself to be slain for the salvation of the guilty even though he was innocent. What is more, the Lord is baptized by his servant, and he who was to give remission of sins, did not wash his own body in the water of regeneration. He fasted for forty days so that others might be fed. He went hungry and fasted so that those who had been starved of the Word and of grace might be filled with the bread of heaven. He withstood the temptation of the devil and was content that his victory should be achieved by no more than words. He did not rule his disciples in the manner in which masters usually exercise their power, but treated them with the mild and gentle affection of brotherly love. He did not even scorn to wash the feet of his disciples, and so even though he was their Lord, he offered an example of how a fellow-servant ought to behave toward his companions and equals by the way in which he treated his own servants. Indeed, we should not be amazed at how he treated those who obeyed him, when he could show such extremes of patience in dealing with Judas, giving food to his enemy and, even though he knew that he was his enemy, not exposing him in public, nor refusing the kiss of the traitor. Moreover, what patience and equanimity he showed in his dealings with the Jews! He made the unbelievers yield by persuasion, he softened the ungrateful by giving way, and answered with gentleness those who sought to contradict him, showing clemency with the proud, and humility with his persecutors, and revealing his willingness even at the very hour of his crucifixion and passion to gather into the fold those who had slain the prophets and turned against God.

(6)

Jesus' Infinite Mercy Shows the Degree of His Patience

And at the very moment of his crucifixion and before they had come to the cruelty of death and the shedding of blood, he patiently heard the reproaches and mockery thrown at him and suffered the insult of being spat upon, when only a short time before he had used his own spittle to give a blind man back his sight. And he, in whose name the devil and his angels are at this very moment being scourged, had to suffer being whipped himself. He was crowned with thorns who crowns martyrs with eternal flowers. He was beaten with palms who yields true palms to those who conquer. He was stripped of his human clothes who clothes others with the robe of immortality. He received bitter poison who offers us the food of heaven, and he was given vinegar to drink who brings the cup of salvation. Even though he was innocent, or rather innocence and justice itself, yet he was numbered among criminals. Truth was corrupted by false witnesses, the judge of the future was himself judged and the Word of God was led in silence to the slaughter. And while the stars were confounded before the cross of the Lord and the elements were thrown into confusion, while the earth trembled and the sun drew back the rays of its eyes, he offered no sound or movement and in his passion gave no sign of his majesty. For everything had to be endured without fail up to the very end so that the perfect and complete patience of Christ could reach its full measure.

And, even after all he had suffered, he accepted his

murderers if they converted and came to him and, with the immense patience of salvation, he excludes nobody from his Church. Even the enemies and blasphemers of his name, if they repent of their sin and acknowledge the crimes they have committed, are admitted not only to the forgiveness of their sin but are given the reward of the kingdom of heaven. What could be more generous or patient than this? Even the one who shed Christ's blood can be renewed by it. Such is the nature of Christ's patience. (Indeed, had it been other than this the Church would not have had Paul as an apostle.)

(7-8)

Imitating Jesus

And so if we too, my dear brothers and sisters, are with Christ and are in Christ and have entered Christ, if he is the way of our salvation, then let us follow Christ's steps on the way of salvation and walk in the example of Christ, as John the apostle instructs us, saying: "He who claims that he is with Christ ought himself to walk as he walked." And Peter on whom the Church was founded by the will of the Lord says the same in his epistle: "Christ suffered for us and left behind him an example that you should follow in his steps, he who did no sin and across whose lips no deceit ever crossed; who was reviled but did not respond, who suffered but did not offer threats, but handed himself over to the one who had unjustly judged him."

(9)

Patience in the Old Testament

We find in the patriarchs and prophets and all those righteous people who prefigure Christ, that they guarded none of their virtues more closely than their patience and their equilibrium.

Abel was the first to initiate and consecrate martyrdom in its origin as the suffering of a just man when he offered no resistance against his brother who was about to kill him but, with humility and mildness, let himself be killed. Abraham who believed in God and was laying down the roots and foundations of his faith, was tested with his son, and did not hesitate or delay to obey the commands of God with the absolute patience of devotion. Isaac, who had been formed to be an image of God's sacrifice and brought to the altar to be slaughtered, won honor by his complete patience. When Jacob was driven out by his brother he left his country with patience; and he showed even greater patience afterwards when as a suppliant he won him over, even though he was now more impious and hostile, with the gifts of peace. Joseph after he had been sold and banished by his brothers not only patiently pardoned them but with generosity and compassion brought them gifts of corn when they came to him. Moses, who was repeatedly reviled by his ungrateful and faithless people and was almost stoned by them, showed his patience and gentleness in the prayers he offered to God on their behalf. David from whom the birth of Christ arose in the flesh, displayed a great and wonderful Christian patience on those numerous occasions when he had it within his power to kill King Saul who was seeking to destroy him. For when he had finally captured Saul, he chose to help rather than exact punishment from him and, even more remarkably, to avenge his eventual murderers.

Many prophets were slain, many martyrs were honored by glorious deaths, all of whom won divine rewards by their praise of patience. For the rewards of grief and passion cannot be won unless patience has preceded that pain and suffering.

So that we shall know, my dear brothers and sisters, with greater clarity and detail how useful and necessary patience is, let us consider that sentence of God which Adam, who was forgetful of the commandment and transgressed the law which had been given him, received at the very beginning of the world and the human race. We learn from him how patient we must be in this life where we are born to struggle with its pressures and conflicts. "Because," he says, "you have paid heed to the voice of your wife, and have eaten from the tree which I commanded you not to eat, I curse the ground for your works. In sorrow and pain will you extract food from it for the whole of your life. It shall bring forth thorns and thistles, and you shall eat the produce of the land, and you will sweat to produce your daily bread until you return to the ground from where you arose. For you are made of dust and into dust you shall return."

We are all bound and constricted by this chain until death wipes us off this earth and we take our leave. For all our days we are bound by necessity to grief and pain, and forced to earn our daily bread by the sweat of our work.

(10-11)

Bearing the Pains of This Life

Each one of us, when we are born and received into this world, begins with tears and, even though we are ignorant and know nothing, yet in the very first hours of birth we know what it is to shed tears. By the providence of nature we weep at the anxieties of human life, and by its crying and wailing our inexperienced soul bears witness to the perils and storms that it is entering. For as long as this life lasts there is effort and toil, and there can be no consolations to help those undergoing them except patience.

While this is helpful and necessary for everyone, it is especially so for us who are more shaken by the devil. We have to fight him in the front line each day, suffering exhaustion in these battles with our inveterate and experienced enemy. In addition to the various and unceasing battles of temptation, we have also in our persecutions to suffer the loss of our inheritance, the terrors of prison, being put in irons, being put to death, the sword, wild beasts, fires and crosses. In short, every sort of torment and pain is ours to be endured in faith and the virtue of patience.

The Lord himself instructs us and says: "These things I have told you so that you may find peace in me, though in this world you will find nothing but pain. Yet have courage for I have overcome the world." But if we who have turned our back on the devil and this world suffer the afflictions of the devil and the world more often and more violently, then how much greater is our need to show that patience whose constant help and companionship will enable us to bear everything that is thrown at us?

(12)

Persevere to Have the Fruit of Virtue

These are saving precepts of our Lord and master: "He that endures until the end will be saved," and "If you continue in my word you will truly be my followers and you shall know the truth and the truth will set you free." We must endure and persevere, my dear brothers and sisters, so that, having been admitted to the hope of truth and liberty, we may finally be able to find truth and liberty itself. For that is what gives us Christians our faith and hope.

But we must show patience so that hope and faith may be brought to fruition. For our glory is not to be sought here and now but in the life to come; as the apostle says: "We are saved by hope, but the hope that is seen is not hope, for what you can see cannot be what you hope for. But if we hope for that we do not see, then we must do it by patience." Therefore waiting and patience are necessary so that we may complete what we have begun to be, and so that we may receive what we believe and hope for when God gives it.

Finally, in another place the divine apostle instructs the righteous and those that do good works and who, by so doing, are laying up treasure in heaven for themselves which will be increased by the payment of divine interest, teaching them to be patient, saying: "While we still have time let us do good to all, especially to those who are in the household of faith. But let us not fail in doing just works, for in due time we shall reap the rewards." He warns us that no one should fail to do good works through impatience. No one, either by being distracted or overcome by temptations, should hesitate half way along the path to praise and glory, allowing what has been accomplished to be lost and what had been begun to be left incomplete. As it is written: "The righteousness of the righteous shall not liberate him on the day when he shall wander from the true path." And again: "Hold fast to that which you have, so that another shall not take your prize from you."

This voice warns us to persevere in patience and strength, so that we who now are on the verge of winning the prize may exercise the enduring patience that will enable us finally to take it.

(13)

Patience a Protection from Evil

But patience, my dear brothers and sisters, not only preserves what is good: it repels what is evil. Favorable to the Holy Spirit, and in harmony with what is celestial and divine, it struggles by its power of resistance against those actions of the flesh and body by which the soul is overcome and captured. Let us now consider just a few examples from many which will serve to illuminate the others. Adultery, deceit, murder are mortal crimes. Let the heart be strengthened and fortified by patience, so that neither the sanctified body nor the temple of God is polluted by adultery. Nor should that innocence which has been dedicated to righteousness be stained with the contagion of deceit. Nor should the hand which has taken the eucharist be besmirched with the sword and bloodshed.

(14)

Love Does Not Exist without Patience

L ove is the bond of fellowship, the foundation of peace, the link and strength of unity. It is greater than both faith and hope. It comes before both good works and martyrdoms, and since it is eternal it will always remain with us in God's presence in the realms of heaven. But if you remove patience, love no longer endures. Remove the substance of endurance and tolerance and it has no roots or strength to persevere. For this reason the apostle spoke about love in the same breath as tolerance and patience. "Love," he says, "is worthy of a great soul, love is kind, love does not envy, nor is it full of pride, it does not rise in anger or think any evil, but is content with all things, believes in all things, finds hope in all things and endures all things." Thus he shows how it is able to persevere, since it knows how to endure all things. And in another place he says: "Sustaining one another in love, striving to keep the unity of the Spirit in the bond of peace." He showed that neither unity nor peace can be preserved unless we love one another with mutual understanding and guard the bond of harmony by the mediation of patience.

It is patience and endurance that enables us not to swear or curse, not to recover things taken from us, to receive a blow and turn our cheek to our attacker, to forgive a brother who sins against us not seventy times seven but absolutely all his sins, to love and pray for our enemies and persecutors. Stephen showed just such patience when he was stoned by the violence of the Jews, and he sought not revenge for himself but pardon for his murderers saying: "Lord, lay not this sin to their charge." Such was the noble end to the first martyr of Christ who, in foreshadowing future martyrs in a glorious death, did not only preach the passion of the Lord, but also imitated his most patient gentleness.

What should I say of that anger, discord, or hatred, which should not be present in a Christian? If true patience is in our heart, then these will not be able to find room within it, or if they attempt to enter, they will soon be excluded and forced to leave, so that the heart shall continue to be a place of peace where the God of peace loves to dwell. The apostle warns us and teaches us saying: "Do not grieve the Holy Spirit to whom you were consigned until the day of redemption. Cast out all your bitterness and anger and indignation and empty noise and blasphemy." For if a Christian has escaped from all the rage and strife of the flesh as from the tempests of the sea, and has now entered in gentleness and tranquility the port of Christ, then we should keep our hearts free from all anger and discord, for we must neither return evil with evil, nor bear hatred to anyone.

(15-16)

Enduring Physical Pain

And furthermore patience is absolutely necessary for all those various illnesses of the flesh and the frequent and severe pains of the body by which the human race is worn down and racked each day. Since in that first transgression of the divine commandment, the strength of the body departed together with immortality, and weakness came with death, so strength cannot be recovered until immortality is recovered. Therefore we are forced to struggle and wrestle with the weakness and frailty of our bodies, which can only be endured with great patience.

In this testing examination many pains are applied, and many kinds of trial are inflicted upon us in the loss of our possessions, the heat of fevers, the dreadful pain of wounds and the death of our friends. Nor indeed is there any clearer way of distinguishing the righteous from the unrighteous than by observing that it is the unrighteous who complain in adversity and blaspheme in their impatience, while it is their patience that reveals the righteous to be true. Thus it is written: "Endure your pain, and have patience in your lowly position, for gold and silver are tested in the fire."

(17)

The Problems of Impatience

And so, my dear brothers and sisters, that the advantage of patience may shine out more brightly, let us consider the troubles which its opposite, impatience, can bring. For just as patience is Christ's blessing, so impatience is the devil's curse. And just as they in whom Christ lives and abides are found to be patient, so the impatient person is someone whose mind is possessed by the wickedness of the devil.

But let us consider the very beginning. The devil was impatient that humanity had been made in the likeness of God. This was the first reason for the fall and destruction. Adam by his impatience ignored the commandment of God and fell to his own death; that is, he did not preserve divine grace by employing the guardianship of patience. Cain too was led to slay his brother by his impatience at his sacrifice and offering. And Esau fell from great to small and lost his primacy through his impatient desire for beans! Was it not by the sin of impatience that the People of Israel in their ingratitude and lack of faith toward the blessings of God first wandered from God? For they were not even prepared to tolerate that Moses should be away from them for a single day in his meeting with God, and they dared to ask for false gods, an ox's head and an image of earth which they could call their guides for their journey. Nor could they restrain their impatience at the instruction and warnings of God until, once they had managed to kill the prophets and every righteous man, they rushed headlong to the cross and to the shedding of the Lord's blood. And similarly it is impatience that produces those who break from orthodox belief within the Church and who, in their rebellion against the peace and love of Christ, are driven into furious hatreds.

In short, we can say that whereas patience produces glory, impatience leads only to ruin.

(19)

The Advantages of Patience

And so, my dear brothers and sisters, having carefully weighed up both the benefits of patience and the evils of impatience, let us hold fast with every means to that patience through which we remain with Christ, in order that we may be able to come with Christ to God. And let our patience be both generous and manifold; let it be neither short-lived nor half-hearted.

The rich virtues of patience flow forth everywhere, rising like a fountain that has a single name and gushing forth in myriad streams through the many ways of glory. Nothing that does not arise from this source can be of such importance to us in our actions for increasing our praise. It is patience that commends us and preserves us before God. It is this that restrains anger, bridles the tongue, governs the mind, guards the peace, regulates discipline, curbs the onrush of desire, calms the violence of pride, quenches the fires of hatred, controls the power of the rich, comforts the poor, maintains the integrity of virgins, keeps widows chaste, ensures the singleness of love in those who are married, makes us humble in prosperity, courageous in adversity, gentle toward insults and injuries.

It teaches the need to pardon those who offend, teaches the offender always to seek forgiveness, conquers temptations, endures persecutions, and brings sufferings for faith and martyrdoms to their completion. It is this that firmly strengthens the foundations of our faith. It is this that gives growth to our hope. This guides our conduct so that we are able to keep to the way of Christ while we walk according to his long-suffering, and makes us continue to be the children of God by imitating the patience of our Father.

(20)

Be Patient Because Judgement Belongs to God

I know, however, my dear brothers and sisters, that there are many people who, because of the number of painful injuries they have received, are determined to take revenge on those who have raged with violence against them, and will not put off the final settlement of these crimes until the day of the last judgement. But I exhort you, while we are still tossed by the storms of this turbulent world, and persecuted by Jews, Gentiles or heretics, to await the day of vengeance with patience. Do not rush to gain a premature retribution for what we have suffered.

For it is written: "Wait for that day," says the Lord, "when I shall rise up in testimony, for my judgement shall be made on every nation when I shall seize the kings and show my anger toward them." Thus the Lord commands us to wait, my dear brothers and sisters, and to show patience as we wait for that day of final retribution which is to come. In the Apocalypse he speaks and says this: "Do not seal up what is written in this book, for now the time is at hand to destroy those who have continued to persecute us, and to besmirch those who have themselves committed filthy acts, and for the righteous to do deeds that are even more righteous, and for those who are pure to increase their purity. Behold I come quickly and my reward is with me to give to all according to their actions." And so the martyrs that cry out and demand vengeance in the outpouring of their grief are required to wait with patience until the end of time when everything shall be fulfilled.

"And when," he says, "he had opened the fifth seal, I saw under the altar of God the souls of those that had been slain for the Word of God and for their witness, and they cried out in a loud voice saying, 'How long, Lord, holy and true, do you refrain from exercising your judgement in vengeance upon those who dwell on earth?' And to each of them was given white robes, and it was said to them that they should rest for a short time until the number of their fellow-servants and brothers and sisters should be reached who were to die after their example."

The Holy Spirit speaking through the prophet Malachi has told us that divine retribution shall come for the shedding of the blood of the just when he said: "Behold the day of the Lord comes like the heat of a kiln, and all the unbelievers and the wicked shall be smashed down like stubble, the day that is to come shall burn them up, so says the Lord."

Similarly we read in the psalms about the advent of God the judge who will be awesome in the majesty of his inquisition: "God shall be made manifest, our God will not remain silent. A fire shall burn before him and a whirlwind shall surround him. He shall call on the heavens above, and the earth below, so that he can separate his people. He will gather the saints together and those who have made a covenant with him by their sacrifices, and the heavens will declare his righteousness; for God is judge."

And Isaiah declares that these same things will take place when he says: "For behold the Lord will come like a fire, and his chariot like a tempest to render vengeance in anger, for they shall be judged by the fire of the Lord, and with his sword they will be struck." And again: "The Lord God of hosts shall stride forth and finish the battle, he shall stir up the battle and shall cry out against his enemies in his strength. I have been silent, shall I always remain silent?"

(21-22)

Leave Vengeance to the Patient Lord

The Lord was silent when he was led like a sheep to the slaughter, or like a lamb silent before its shearer. He did not cry out or raise his voice in the streets. He showed no reluctance or resistance when he offered his back for beating, and his cheeks to other men's palms, nor did he turn his face away from the foulness of being spat on. Nor, when he was accused by the chief priests and scribes, did he offer any reply. And, while Pilate deliberated, he remained patient in his silence. This is the same person who, having remained silent in his passion, will break his silence when he gives judgement. This is our God, who is known to be God not by everyone but only by those who believe and have faith. When he is made manifest in his second coming he will not keep silent, for whereas he was hidden by his humility at the first, at the second he shall come in the clear light of his power.

Let us wait for him, my dear brothers and sisters, our judge and avenger, who, when he takes vengeance, will be taking vengeance not only for himself but also for the people of his Church and the company of all righteous people from the beginning of the world. He who hastens to take his own vengeance should remember that the avenger has not yet been avenged. In the Apocalypse the angel refuses to allow John's wish to worship him and says: "Look, do not do this, because I am your fellowservant and the servant of your brothers and sisters. It is Jesus whom you should worship."

How great is the patience of our Lord Jesus who is worshipped in heaven, but is not yet avenged here on earth! Let us consider his patience, my dear brothers and sisters, in our own persecutions and sufferings. And, in the firm expectation of his arrival, let us show our obedience to him. Let us not, since we are servants before God, seek to rush forward with a profane and immodest haste but rather let us press on in our struggle and remain vigilant with all our heart and stay true to the Lord's commandments in all our suffering. So that, when the day of anger and vengeance arrives, we may not suffer punishment with the ungodly and the sinners, but receive honor among the righteous and those who fear God.

(23-24)

On Works and Alms

Grace, the Basis of Works

Many and great are the divine gifts, my dear brothers and sisters, in which the plentiful and abundant mercy of God our Father and Christ has been and shall continue to be exercised for our salvation. For the Father sent his Son to save and enliven us and so to restore us, and he sent his Son, who wished to be the Son of Man so that he could make us all the sons of God. He made himself humble so that he could lift up a people who were fallen; he was wounded so that he might heal our wounds; he was a slave so that he might lead other slaves to their freedom. He suffered death so that he might show mortals immortality.

These are the many and great gifts of divine mercy. But even more than this is the providence and kindness which, by saving means, has ensured that even after we have received redemption, there are further ways for us to find salvation. For when our master came, and had healed the wounds that Adam had brought and had cured the poisons of the old serpent, he laid down a law for the man whom he had healed, warning him not to sin any more or he would suffer a much greater punishment. And so we were trapped and confined by the command of innocence. For the weakness and helplessness of our human fragility would not have been able to accomplish anything unless divine pity had come to our aid once again and opened up the way of salvation by directing us to works of justice and mercy. Thus by showing generosity to others we are able to wash away any new impurity.

(1)

Cleanliness of Heart

The Holy Spirit speaks in the divine scriptures and says: "Sins are cleansed by alms and faith." This does not refer to those sins committed previously since these have been cleansed by the blood and sanctification of Christ. Similarly he says: "Just as water puts out fire, so alms put out sin." Here too it is shown and laid down that just as the water of salvation puts out the fire of hell, so alms and good deeds extinguish the flames of sin. And just as baptism gives remission of sins once and for all, so the constant and unending doing of good work is like baptism and dispenses the generosity of God's gifts for a second time.

This too our master teaches in the gospels. For when it had been brought to his attention that his disciples had begun eating without having first washed their hands, he said in reply: "He who made the outside made the inside too. Give alms and all of you will be made clean." Thus he taught that it was not your hands which should be washed but rather your heart and that uncleanness must be removed from the inside rather than from the outside. For they who have cleansed their inner selves have also cleansed what is outside, and they whose mind has been cleansed have also begun to purify their skin and body. And furthermore, by pointing out to us how we may be cleansed and purged, he urges us to give alms. In his mercy he teaches and warns us to be merciful, and because he seeks to help those he redeemed at great cost, he tells us that those who after baptism have become unclean may be cleansed once again.

(2)

Spiritual Healing

Therefore let us acknowledge, dear brothers and sisters, the healing gift of divine compassion, and since none of us can be without some wounds in our conscience, let us care for our wounds with spiritual healing. Let no one flatter themselves that their heart is so pure and spotless that they can rely on their innocence and think that they have no need of medicine. For it is written: "Who shall boast of a pure heart or claim that he is free of sins?" And again in his epistle John sets it down and says: "If we say we have no sin then we are deceiving ourselves and are not in possession of the truth." But if no one can be without sin and whoever says that they are blameless is either proud or stupid, then how necessary and plentiful is the compassion of God who, in recognizing that those who have been healed are still not immune from wounds, created saving remedies that would allow these wounds to be healed and cured!

(3)

Works of Mercy

Never, dearest brothers and sisters, has divine instruction failed in always and everywhere pressing the people of God to works of mercy; never has it been silent on this, whether in the Old or the New Testament. By the sounds and urgings of the Holy Spirit, everyone is given the hope of the heavenly kingdom and commanded to give alms. The God of Isaiah demands and ordains: "Cry out as loudly as you can and do not spare yourself: raise your voice like a trumpet and proclaim to my people their sins, and to the house of Jacob their crimes." And when he had ordered that they should be reproached for their sins and when he exposed their sins to the full force of his anger and told them that even if they cried and begged and fasted they could not atone for their sins, and that not even if they rolled in sackcloth and ashes would they mollify the anger of God, yet in the end he said that it was only by alms that God could be placated, saying: "Break your bread with the man who is hungry and bring the destitute into your house. If you see one who is naked then give him clothing and do not despise the household of your own seed. Then shall your light shine forth like the dawn and your sanctification shall emerge at once and justice shall go before you and the light of God will surround you; you shall cry out, and he will say, 'Here I am.' "

(4)

Give Your Goods Away

Thus in the gospel the Lord, who is our teacher of life and master of our eternal salvation, who gives life to all those who believe and stands by them forever, enjoins and demands in his divine commandments nothing so often as that we should apply ourselves to giving alms; that we should not brood over the possessions we have on earth but rather should seek to store up treasures in heaven. For he says: "Sell all your possessions and give alms," and again: "Do not store up treasures on earth, where they will be eaten away by moths and rust, and where thieves will break in and steal them. For where your treasure is, there will your heart be also." And when he wanted to show someone who observed the law how to become perfect and complete, he said: "If you really want to be perfect then go off and sell everything you have and give it to the needy and you will have treasure in heaven, and come and follow me."

Similarly in another place he says that anyone who is a merchant of eternal grace and trader of eternal salvation, ought to sell all their goods in order to purchase out of their estate a precious pearl; that is, eternal life for which the price is Christ's blood. "The kingdom of heaven," he says, "is like a precious pearl which a merchant seeks and once he finds it sells everything he has to buy it."

Those he sees who are committed to helping and nourishing the poor he calls the sons of Abraham. For when Zacchaeus said: "Look, I shall give half of my goods to the poor and if I have cheated anyone I shall repay them fourfold," Jesus replied: "This day salvation is ful-

71

filled in this house, since he too is a son of Abraham."
For if Abraham believed in God and was regarded as just,
then surely anyone who follows the teaching of God and
gives alms also believes in God; and they who have the
truth of faith, preserve the fear of God; and whoever
preserves the fear of God, considers God by showing
compassion to the poor. They act in this way because
they believe, because they know, that the precepts written down are true to God and that the holy scriptures
cannot lie; that barren trees, that is those people who
bear no fruit, are cut down and thrown into the fire, but
that the merciful are called to the kingdom. In another
place those who do good works and are fruitful he calls
faithful but says that those who are unfruitful and barren
have no faith: "If you have not been faithful in unjust
mammon, then who will trust you with the truth? If you
have not been faithful with that which belongs to someone else then who will give you what is your own?"

(7-8)

Do Not Fear to Be Generous

But if you are worried and are afraid that by devoting yourself wholly to works of charity you will be reduced to poverty by the generosity of your giving, then you do not need to be afraid since you are secure. That which is spent for Christ and which facilitates the work of heaven can never be used up. This promise I make to you not on my own authority but supported by the pledge of God. The Holy Spirit spoke through Solomon saying: "He who gives to the poor will never be in need, but he who turns his eye away will be in great poverty," showing that those who are merciful and charitable cannot fall into want, but rather that the miserly and the barren will afterwards find themselves poverty-stricken. The same is said by the blessed apostle Paul when, full of the grace of divine inspiration, he said: "He who gives seed to the sower and offers bread to the hungry, will multiply your seed and increase the fruit of your justice, so that you will be enriched in all things." And again: "The administration of this service shall not only supply the needs of the saints, but shall flow by the many acts of thanks to the Lord."

For thanks for our almsgiving and good deeds are given by the poor to God and are measured and rewarded by him. And the Lord in the gospel, already weighing the hearts of such people, and denouncing those who are faithless and unbelieving, says with a prophetic voice: "Do not think about what you are to eat or drink or wear. For this is what the faithless think. Your Father knows that you need all these. Seek first of all the kingdom and justice of God, and everything else will be added to you."

73

Everything will be given, he says, to those who seek the kingdom and justice of God; for God says that when the day of judgement comes those who will be admitted to the kingdom will be those who did good works in his Church.

(9)

Do Not Love Money

Therefore do not fear that all your resources will suddenly disappear if you give too generously, since if you are a miser and absorbed in fear for the depletion of your goods, you will find that life and salvation itself will have been lost to you. While you are consumed by fear for your estate, you fail to see that you yourself are wasting away and that you are a lover of mammon rather than of your soul, and you will find that you have sacrificed yourself for it. It is with this in mind that the apostle cries out and says: "We bring nothing into this world, and can take nothing away from it. Let us be content with food and clothing. Anyone who wants to become rich will fall into temptation and be snared by a multitude of harmful desires which will drown him in damnation and destruction. For the root of all evil is the love of money. Those who seek it are shipwrecked from their faith and embroiled in many troubles."

(10)

Providence Will Care for You

Do you really fear that your estate will fail if you begin to use it for charitable works? When has a just person ever wanted for means to live? For it is written: "The Lord will not kill the just with hunger." When Elijah was alone he was helped and fed by the ravens; when Daniel had been thrown into the lion's den he was provided with food from God. Do you think that when you do good works and earn the Lord's favor that you will lack for food? He himself in the gospel reproaches those who are of wavering mind and little faith, and says in evidence: "Look at the birds of the sky, they do not sow nor do they reap, nor harvest into granaries, and yet your Father feeds them. Surely you are better than them?" God feeds the birds, and provides food for the sparrows, and even those creatures which are not conscious of the divine do not lack for food and drink. Do you think that as a Christian, as a servant of God, as one given to good works, and so dear to God, that you will ever be in need?

You could only think like that if you believed that one who gives food to Christ will not be fed by Christ or that those who are given heavenly and divine things will lack earthly ones. From where could such an unbelieving or sacrilegious thought come? What is such a faithless heart doing in the house of faith? How could someone who does not believe wholly in Christ be called a Christian? Pharisee would be a more appropriate name. For when the Lord in the gospel spoke about the giving of alms and told us faithfully and with our salvation in mind that we should use our earthly resources intelligently in order to make friends who will afterwards receive us into eternal homes, scripture says further: "But the Pharisees, who were very covetous, heard all these things, and derided him." Even now we see some in the Church whose deaf ears and closed hearts do not allow the light of spiritual warnings to enter them.

(11-12)

Riches, a Burden to the Soul

Why do you concern yourself with these empty and foolish thoughts as if you were prevented from doing good works by your fear and concern for the future? Why do you make these shadowy and deceitful excuses? Confess the truth because God who knows all things cannot be deceived, and draw these secrets hidden in your mind out into the light of day. The shadows of barrenness have taken control of your mind, and the light of truth has departed from it, and a deep and profound night of avarice has blinded your carnal breast. You are a slave and captive to your money, bound by the chains and ties of greed; and, after Christ set you free, you have returned once more to your imprisonment. You save up money, which though it is saved does not save you; you amass a fortune whose weight only burdens you with an even heavier load; you have forgotten the answer that God made to the rich man, who boasted with foolish exultation in the abundance of his overflowing capital: "You fool," he said, "on this very night your soul will be demanded from you. What use will all your possessions be?" Why do you brood alone over your wealth in your solitude? Why do you increase your estate to your own detriment when all you are doing is making yourself richer in the goods of this world but poorer in the eyes of God? Divide your profits with God and share your gains with Christ: make Christ a shareholder of your earthly possessions, so that he also may make you his co-heir in the kingdom of heaven.

(13)

Buy Gold from Christ

You are making a big mistake and deceiving yourself if you think yourself rich in this world. Listen to the voice of your Lord in the Apocalypse, rebuking such people with just reproaches: "You think," he says, "that you are rich, and wealthy and that you lack nothing; and yet you are ignorant of the fact that you are wretched and miserable and poor and blind and naked. I suggest that you buy my gold hardened in the fire, and white cloth so that you may clothe yourself and not appear in the full shame of your nakedness; and anoint your eyes with eye lotion so that you can see." And so you who are wealthy and rich, buy from Christ gold tried in the fire, so that your dross being removed as if by fire, you may yourself become pure gold purged by your alms and just actions. Buy your white cloth so that you who according to Adam were naked and unsightly may wear the white clothes of Christ.

(14)

The Rich Shamed by the Example of the Poor

But as you are now, you cannot exercise charity in the Church. For eyes clouded with shadows of blackness and shrouded in night cannot see the needy and poor. You who are rich and wealthy think that you celebrate the feast of the Lord when you are completely ignorant of the offering; you come into the Lord's house without a sacrifice, and receive no part of that sacrifice which the poor have offered.

Remember the widow in the gospel who, taking to heart the teaching of heaven, gave alms in spite of her difficult and pressing situation and cast the two small coins into the treasury, which were all she had. When the Lord saw her he judged her good deed not by its amount, but by the intention, and considered not how much she had given, but her total means. He said in response: "I say to you that this widow has contributed more than all those others to the offerings of God; for all these have given out of their abundance into the gifts of God; but she out of her poverty has given everything she had."

What a fine and fortunate woman, who even before the day of judgement was worthy of the Judge's attention! Let the rich be ashamed of their barrenness and lack of belief; she, a widow, a poor widow, is found to be overflowing in her charity. And whereas everything which is given is usually bestowed on widows and orphans, she gave when she had the right to receive. Thus from this example we may know just how great the punishment will be for those who are rich and ungenerous since even the poor are urged to exercise charity. And so that we may understand that these works are given to God, and that whoever performs them gains the Lord's favor, Christ speaks of the "gifts of God." He indicates that the widow cast her two coins into the "gifts of God." Thus it is made even clearer, that they who have pity upon the poor lend to God.

(15)

Putting Christ in First Place

Nor, my dear brothers and sisters, should Christians be checked and held back from just works, nor should they think themselves excused because they have children. For, in religious expenditure, we ought to think first of Christ, who in any case says that he will receive children.

As he himself teaches and warns: "He that loves his father or mother more than me, is not worthy of me." Similarly in Deuteronomy the same things are written about the strength of faith and the love of God: "Those who say to their father or mother, I have not known you, and who do not acknowledge their children, these have observed your words and kept the covenant." For if we love God with all our heart, we ought to put God before either our parents or our children.

John in his epistle says that there is no love of God in those who do not exercise alms to the poor. "Whoever," he says, "has worldly possessions and sees that his brother is in need and closes his heart to him, how can the love of God be inside him?" For giving alms to the poor is a lending to God; and what is given to the least, is given to Christ, earthly things must not by anyone be preferred to heavenly, nor must human things be more valued than divine.

(16)

Give and There Will Be Gifts for You

We can take the example of the widow in the First Book of Kings, when everything had been consumed in the drought and famine, and she had made her ash-baked bread out of the meal and oil that remained. She was preparing to die with her children when Elijah arrived and asked that he be fed first. Only then what was left should be given to herself and her children to eat. She did not hesitate to obey him, and even though she was a mother who was hungry and in need, she put Elijah before her children.

In God's sight an act was done to please him, and what was asked for was given immediately and freely and moreover was given not from an abundance but from a meager store. While her children were starving another was given preference, and neither hunger nor need were allowed to prevail over mercy. And while the bodily life was despised in this action, the life of the soul was saved. Elijah therefore, who prefigures Christ, showed that Christ, according to his loving mercy, renders to each their recompense, by answering: "The Lord says, 'The vessel of meal shall not fail, and the container of oil shall not run dry, until the day when the Lord gives rain upon the earth.' "

According to the faith of divine promise, those things which she gave were multiplied. And her just action and the mercy she showed produced their own increase and accumulation, and the vessels of meal and oil were measured out to her in full.

Nor did the mother rob her children of that which she gave to Elijah, but rather conferred upon her children that which she did bountifully and piously. And she did not even know Christ, nor had she heard of his teaching, nor was she redeemed by his cross and passion, and yet she did what she did. Thus it is clear from this just how much they offend Christ who put themselves and their children before Christ and save up their wealth instead of sharing their plenteous riches with those who are in the greatest need.

(17)

Care for Your Children's Prosperity

Do not think that as the father of your children you should be a temporary and weak one, but be rather as strong as he who is the eternal and abiding Father of spiritual sons and daughters. You should assign that wealth of yours which you are saving for your heirs to him. Let him be the guardian, him the executor for your children, let him be in divine majesty their protector, against all the injuries of this world. Property which is entrusted to God will not be confiscated by the state, nor will it be taxed by the exchequer nor subject to the law. A heritage which is put under the guardianship of God will remain safe and secure. This is indeed to provide for the children you love into the time ahead; this is to provide for your future heirs with all the piety of a parent according to the holy scriptures, which say: "I have been young, and now am old, yet I have not seen the just forsaken, nor his children want for bread. All day long he shows mercy and lends, and his children are blessed." And again: "He who walks without reproach to his integrity, shall leave blessed children after him."

Thus you are a false and useless father unless you think sincerely about your children and provide for their welfare with true religious devotion. You who dedicate yourselves to the inheritance on earth rather than in heaven are giving your children to the devil rather than to Christ, and are sinning twice and falling into a twofold and double guilt: in that you do not procure for your children the aid of God their Father, and in that you teach your children to love their inheritance more than Christ.

(19)

Advise Generosity

You should be the sort of father to your children that Tobit was to his. Give the children pledged to your care useful and life-enhancing advice, such as he gave to his son when he said: "And now my son, I tell you to serve God in truth, and do that which will please him, and command your sons to exercise justice and alms, and be mindful of God, and bless his name always." And again: "Remember God on every day of your life and do not transgress his commandments. Act justly every day of your life, and do not walk the paths of injustice, since if you act with truth your works will find respect. Give alms from your goods and do not turn your face from the poor; so will the face of God not be turned from you. Give, my son, according to your means; if you have much then give more alms; if you have little then give from that little, since almsgiving saves from death, and from darkness. For alms are a good gift for all who give them in the sight of the most high God."

(20)

Be Generous in God's Sight

What sort of gift is it, dear brothers and sisters, that is displayed in the presence of God? If when Gentiles make a generous offering, it increases their prestige and glory to have the proconsuls or emperor present (and a more lavish and expensive show is put on by those presenting it so that it will impress the great), then how much greater and more illustrious is the glory of the generous offering, at which God and Christ are present? How much richer must the decorations be and how much larger the expense when the powers of heaven assemble at the spectacle, when the angels assemble, and when the person who presents the show is not a candidate for a four-horse chariot or a consulship, but will receive eternal life; when it is not the empty and transitory favor of the people which is being sought, but the perpetual reward of the kingdom of heaven!

(21)

87

Love Christ in Other People

What greater inducement to good works could Christ offer us than by saying that whatever is given to the needy and poor, is given to himself; and in saying that he is offended, if the needy and poor are not supplied? And so he ensured that anyone who is not moved in church by the sight of their brother or sister may nevertheless be moved by looking on Christ. And also he ensured that anyone who might ignore a fellow-servant who is in difficulties and in need, may still consider the Lord who stands in that rejected person.

And so, dearest brothers and sisters, you who fear the Lord, and who have rejected and trampled underfoot the world and have raised your mind to the highest and most divine things, let us in complete faith, with a devout mind and with works that shall not cease, offer obedience and present ourselves to the Lord. Let us give clothes to Christ on earth so that we may receive the clothing of heaven. Let us offer the meat and drink of this earth so that we may go to the heavenly banquet with Abraham and Isaac and Jacob. And so that we may bring in a great harvest, let us sow plentifully. Let us think of our life and eternal salvation, while there is still time. As Paul the apostle advises and says: "While we have time, let us do good to all, especially to those from the household of faith. But let us not get tired of doing good, for at the appropriate time we shall bring in the harvest."

(23-24)

Common Property

Let us consider, dearest brothers and sisters, what the body of believers did under the apostles when at the beginning the mind was strong in greater virtues, and the faith of the believers was fresh and burned with the flames of faith. They sold their houses and farms, and they freely offered all they had to the apostles for them to distribute among the poor. They sold and distributed their earthly possessions so that they would be able to enjoy the fruits of an eternal estate. And they acquired houses where they were going to live for ever. Such was their abundance in good works and their unity in love. As we read in the Acts of the Apostles: "And the mass of the believers acted with a single mind and soul; they had no difference between them, nor did they think of anything they had as their own, but they held all their goods in common."

This is to become a child of God by a spiritual birth; this is to imitate the fairness of God the Father by a heavenly law. For whatever is of God is common property, nor is anyone to be excluded from his generosity and gifts, so that the whole human race may have an equal share of God's goodness and abundance. Thus it is for everyone alike that day gives its light, the sun its brilliance, the rain its moisture, and the wind its breath. There is one sleep for those who slumber, and a common radiance from the stars and the moon. In this example of equality those on earth who share what they have with their fellow human beings, and who are free and just in their gifts to all, become like God the Father.

(25)

Winning the Palm of Victory

What then, dearest brothers and sisters, will be the glory of those who are charitable? What will be their heights of joy, when the Lord begins to number his people, and distributes the rewards for their merits and good works as he has promised. What will be the joy when he will give the heavenly for the earthly, the eternal for the temporal, and the great for the small? What will be the joy when he will offer us to the Father, who restored us by his sanctification? It is he who will give us the gift of eternal and immortal life which has been offered to us once again by his life-giving blood. It is he who will lead us back to paradise, opening the realms of heaven.

Let us keep these things resolutely in our thoughts. Let us understand them in the fullness of faith. Let us love them with all our heart, and purchase them by that greatness of spirit which is shown in unceasing works. The saving works of generosity, dearest brothers and sisters, are a glorious and divine thing. They are the great consolation of believers, the wholesome safeguard of our security, the defense of hope, the guardian of faith, the medicine for sin, a thing readily done which is both great and easy, a peaceful crown without the peril of persecution, God's true and greatest service to the weak and needy, to the strong and the great.

Let us strive willingly and swiftly with saving deeds for the palm of victory. Let us all compete in the race of justice watched by God and Christ. And since we have now begun to be above this life and the world, let us make our way unimpeded by the desires of this life or the world. If the day of recompense or persecution finds us clothed and quick to respond in running this race of generosity, the Lord will not fail to give us the rewards we deserve. In peace he will give to the conquerors a white crown for our good works and, in persecution, he will give us a purple crown for our passion.

(26)

On the Death Rate

Steadfastness in Adversity

My dear brothers and sisters, I am sure that most of you have managed to keep a steady heart, a firm faith and a devout soul, remaining unmoved by the enormous losses in the present epidemic. I am sure that you have stayed firm like a solid and immovable rock in the face of the great storms of this world and the violent onslaughts of time, withstanding its attacks rather than being overwhelmed. And certainly these trials have served to prove your worth rather than to defeat you. Nevertheless, since I have noticed that some of you, whether from weakness of will, inadequacy of faith, attachment to this life on earth or, most seriously of all, through wandering from the path of truth, remain less steadfast (and do not show the invincible divine strength in their hearts), I think that this matter must not be hidden or passed over in silence. But insofar as our meager capabilities extend, we must in the fullness of our power and armed with the words of our Lord, root out this cowardly and decadent state of mind. Thus they who have begun to be a man or woman of God and of Christ can be seen to be worthy of God and Christ.

(1)

The Closeness
of the Kingdom

My dear brothers and sisters, they who fight for God, and who are stationed in the camp of heaven, and breathe the breath of the divine, ought to stand up and be counted so that in the storms and tempests of this world they may have no fear or trembling. These events were predicted by the Lord who gave us warning so as to prepare and strengthen his Church and enable it to bear everything that was to come; for he prophesied that wars and famines and earthquakes and plagues would strike everywhere. And so that we should not be paralyzed with fear at the onset of a new and unexpected disaster, he warned us that at the end of time these terrible events would increase. Observe that what had been predicted has come to pass and, just as those things have come to pass that were predicted, so those will follow that are promised. The Lord himself gave his word and said: "When you see all these things come to pass, know that the kingdom of God is close at hand."

The kingdom of God, dear brothers and sisters, is now close at hand, the rewards of life, the joy of eternal salvation, perpetual happiness, and the possession of the paradise which was lost only recently, all these are approaching already while this world is passing away. Already heavenly things are succeeding to earthly and great to small and eternal to transient. What place can there be for fear and anxiety? Among these things only someone who lacks both hope and faith could feel terror or regret. The only person who would be frightened of death is someone who does not want to go to Christ. And the only people who do not want to go to Christ are those who do not believe that they are going to reign with Christ.

(2)

Transcending This World

It is written: "The just live by faith." If you are just and live by faith, if you truly believe in God, why (since you will be with Christ and be secure in the promise of the Lord) do you not embrace that call to Christ which is given to you and rejoice that you are delivered from the devil? Simeon, that truly just man who kept to the teaching of the Lord with absolute faith, had been told by the Lord that he would not die before he had seen the Christ. And so when Christ with his mother came into the temple, he recognized in his soul that Christ was born, about whom the prophecy had been made to him, and now that he had seen him, he realized that he was about to die. But he was filled with joy about his imminent death and, secure in the knowledge that he was soon to be called away, embraced the child and blessed God saying: "Lord, now allow your servant to depart in peace in accordance to your word, since my eyes have seen your salvation."

Thus he proved and bore witness that peace, freedom and tranquillity will come to the servants of God when we have escaped the turmoils of this world and at last reach the port of eternal rest and safety, and when we transcend this death and arrive at immortality. This is our peace, this is true serenity, this is the firm and everlasting place of safety.

(3)

Escape from the Sorrow of Temptation

Meanwhile what does this world consist in except the daily battles fought against the devil and all his weapons, in conflict after conflict? Our struggle is with desire for gain, with shamelessness, with anger and ambition, with the vices of the flesh and with the entice-ments of this world, a struggle which is both exhausting and unremitting. Our spirit is besieged and encompassed on every side by the assaults of the devil and is barely able to meet and repel so many attacks at the same time. If avarice has been flattened, then desire rises up; if desire has been held down then ambition gets up; if ambition is regarded as worthless then anger is felt—pride rises up, drunkenness seems inviting, envy severs close bonds, and competition breaks friendships. You are forced to say things forbidden by the law of God, and compelled to take oaths which it does not permit.

So many are the attacks suffered by the soul every day and so many are the dangers which threaten the heart! Do you really want to spend so much time surrounded by the weapons of the devil? Surely we should desire and choose that death should intervene in our aid and quicken our journey to Christ according to his own instruction and word: "Yes indeed I say to you that you will weep and cry but that the world shall rejoice; you will be sad but your grief will turn into joy."

Who does not then desire to be freed from sorrow? Who does not rush to reach joy? And since our sorrow is turned into joy, the Lord himself has told us and said:

"I will see you again, and your heart shall rejoice, and no one will be able to take your joy from you." Since to see Christ is to rejoice, and our only true joy is in seeing Christ, then it can only be blindness of mind and complete madness to love the pressures and pains and tears of this world and not rush to meet that joy which can never be taken away.

(4-5)

God is Trustworthy

This is the situation, my dear brothers and sisters, because there is an absence of faith, because no one believes the promises that God, who is true, has made and whose word to those who believe is firm and everlasting. If any worthy and honorable person were to make you a promise, you would have a firm expectation that you were not about to be deceived by that person whose words and acts you knew and trusted. And yet when it is God who speaks to you, can you really show such little faith and waver in your doubt? God has promised you immortality and eternity when you leave this world, and yet you still feel doubt? This reveals a complete ignorance of God; this is to commit the offence of unbelief before Christ, the master of those who believe; this is to have been placed in the Church and yet to be without faith in the house of faith.

(6)

To Die is Gain

Christ himself, the master of our salvation and well-being, has told us how great the benefit of leaving this world is, when he said in reply to his disciples who had become downhearted at the news that he was about to leave them: "If you really loved me, you would rejoice since I am going to my Father." He showed by this that when those we love and cherish leave this world, we ought to rejoice rather than grieve.

It was in reference to this that the blessed apostle in his letter said: "To me to live is Christ, and to die is gain." For he thought that the greatest gain was to be free of the chains of this life, to be no longer exposed to all the sins and vices of the flesh; to be redeemed from terrible tribulations and, delivered from the poisoned jaws of the devil, to pass at the command of Christ into the joys of everlasting salvation.

(7)

The Suffering of Christians

But there are certain people who have been troubled by the fact that this disease has attacked believers and non-believers alike. It would seem as if the purpose of our whole life as Christians were to enjoy the happiness of this world, and as if we were immune from any contact with its evils, not having to endure all the adversities we meet here. Indeed, it would seem as if our full happiness were not reserved for a future time! Yet what is there in this world which is not common to us all, so long as we all are subject to the same law of birth and thus have the same human body? Even so while we remain on earth, although we may indeed share our bodily form with the rest of humanity, our spiritual form sets us apart. But until this corruptible form becomes incorruptible, and this mortal form obtains immortality and the Spirit guides us to God the Father, we shall share with the rest of humankind whatever troubles of the flesh there are.

When the earth brings forth only sterile fruit, none shall escape famine. When a city is attacked by the enemy and captured, everyone will suffer captivity and destruction. When the skies are clear and without clouds, then everyone shall suffer drought together. And when the ship is dashed to pieces by the craggy rocks, the shipwreck affects every sailor without exception. Diseases of the eyes, attacks of fever, diseases of the limbs, are as common to us as to others, so long as we share this flesh on earth.

Yet if Christians really think and acknowledge the implications of their belief, then they will discover that

103

they have even more to endure in this world than others, because they are conscious of their struggle against the assaults of the devil. The holy scriptures teach and give us fair warning: "My son, when you come to the service of God, remain firm in your sense of justice and fear, and prepare your soul for temptation." And again: "Endure in pain, and show patience in your humility, for gold and silver are tried in the fire."

(8-9)

Patience as Love for God

This exercise of patience is always displayed by the righteous. Such a discipline was always observed by the apostles themselves, who followed the commandment of the Lord not to grumble in adversity, but to accept with strength and patience whatever may happen here on earth.

My dear brothers and sisters, we must not grumble in adversity, but must endure with patience and strength whatever happens, since it is written: "The sacrifice of God is a broken spirit; a contrite and humbled heart God does not despise."

In Deuteronomy too the Holy Spirit advises Moses, and says: "The Lord your God will trouble you, and will force you to starve, and you will know in the depths of your heart whether you have kept his commandments truly or not," and again, "The Lord your God will test you so that he may know whether you love the Lord your God with all your heart and with all your soul."

(11)

Present Evil is Nothing in Comparison to Future Good

Abraham satisfied the Lord because, in his desire to please him, he did not fear to lose his son nor even to carry out the killing himself. You who cannot bear to lose a son by the common fate of death, what would you do if you were commanded to kill your own son? Fear of God and faith ought to make you prepared for anything. If you have lost everything you own, or your limbs are racked by the constant and crippling rage of diseases, or you have lost your wife, your children, or friends and face this painful loss, then do not allow such things to be stumbling-blocks but rather battles. They should not weaken or break the faith of a Christian but rather reveal his or her courage in the struggle; since the power of these evils here and now are as nothing in comparison to the good things which are to come.

There can be no victory without there having been a battle first. Only when victory has been seized in the thick of the fight can the crown be given to the victors. The true pilot is found in the tempest. The true soldier is shown in the fight. When there is no danger the trial is worthless, but when the battle is a serious one, then the testing is real. A tree which has sent down deep roots is not brought down by the winds that lash it. The ship which is firmly anchored is tossed but not broken by the waves. And when the corn is beaten on the threshing floor, the strong and heavy grains despise the wind while the empty chaff is carried up and away upon its gusts.

(12)

Weakness Leads to Strength

Thus the apostle Paul, after being shipwrecked, and beaten and after suffering many terrible tortures, says that he was not cast down but strengthened by his troubles, since these trials served to put him to the test and allowed him to emerge with greater certainty. "I was given," he says, "a goad to my flesh, the angel of Satan, who struck me so that I should not rise up; and three times I called on the Lord to rid me of it. And he said to me, 'My grace is enough for you; for strength is made perfect by weakness.' " And so when weakness and inadequacy creep up upon us, it is then that our strength is made perfect. Faith, if it has remained firm in the trial, is crowned, as is written: "The kiln proves the potter's works; and just men the trial of tribulation."

This then is the difference between us and those who do not know God, that they complain and grumble in adversity while we are not diverted from the true path of virtue and faith but are made even stronger in the midst of suffering.

(13)

Embracing Suffering

This present trial in which the strength of the body is drained by an inward flux, and fire in the marrow breaks out in sores upon the jaws, the insides are shaken by continual vomiting, the eyes made bloodshot by fever, the feet or some other parts of the body removed through the action of putrid disease, while from the weakness occasioned in this maiming and waste of the body, either motion is impeded, or hearing impaired or sight lost—even this trial can become an example of faith.

What greatness of spirit it is to battle with the soul unshaken against these assaults of desolation and death! How glorious to stand unbowed among the ruins of the human race, instead of lying prostrate with those who have no hope in God! We should be joyful, and embrace with gladness what the occasion grants us, namely, that in the firm exercise of our faith and, by bearing our suffering on the hard road to Christ, we are accepting the reward of his way and faith, which he himself will judge.

Fear of death is for those who have not been spiritually reborn by baptism and are destined for the flames of hell. Fear of death is for those who are not part of the passion of Christ on the cross. Fear of death is for those whose death here will be followed by a second death. Fear of death is for those who will suffer the torments of a flame which will never cease after they have passed from this world.

(14)

Good from Evil

But, my dear brothers and sisters, the relevance and necessity of this plague which now appears so full of terrors and savagery is that it is a trial of the righteousness of each of us, and weighs our spirits in the balance. It will prove whether those of us who are healthy tend to the sick, whether relatives show the love they ought to their own, whether masters show pity toward their sick servants, whether doctors avoid the sick who are crying out for their help, whether the violent suppress their ferocity, whether the greedy can have the fire of their insatiable desire for wealth quenched by their fear of death, whether the arrogant can learn humility, whether the shameless can soften their recklessness, whether the rich, when they have lost their own children and realize that they are going to die without any heirs, will finally show some generosity and distribute their wealth. If this plague has brought no other benefit, it will have done much service to Christians and the servants of God by teaching us not to be afraid of death and by turning our attention toward the desire for martyrdom. To us such things are testing grounds, not deaths. They inspire the mind with courage and glory and, by forcing us to disregard death, they prepare us to receive the crown of victory.

(16)

Desire to Live in the Kingdom

We ought to remember that we should do not our own will but the will of God. This is what the Lord has commanded us to pray each day. How absurd and perverse it would be if we pray that God's will may be done and yet, when God calls us out of this world, we should hesitate to obey his will. We refuse and show reluctance and, like stubborn servants, we have to be dragged into the presence of our Lord with cries of protest, seeming to depart under duress rather than out of choice. So, we want to be honored by his celestial gifts, yet we come to him against our will. But why then do we pray and ask for the coming of the kingdom of heaven, if we are so captivated by the delights of this earth? Why is it that we ask again and again that the day of the kingdom may come soon, if what we really desire and wish for is that we should serve the devil here on earth and not that we should rule with Christ?

(18)

There is Life After Death

How many times has it been revealed even to us, who are insignificant in the extreme, and how frequently and clearly have I, by God's will, been directed to protest and declare in public that we should not feel sad for those of our brothers and sisters, who at the Lord's command, have been freed from their life here on earth. We know that they have not been lost but rather sent on ahead. In leaving us they are but showing the way, as people often do on a journey or upon a voyage. We ought to show affection rather than sorrow, and we should not dress in black when they have already taken on clothes of white. For we should not give the unbelievers cause to make the just and deserved reproach that, while we claim that they live on with God, yet we mourn them as if they were extinct and dead for ever, and that the faith which we manifest in our language and speech is contradicted by the testimony of our feelings and thoughts. In so doing we are destroying our own faith and hope, and making those things we affirm appear the flimsiest piece of fiction. It is useless to proclaim virtue in our words and then destroy it by our actions.

The apostle Paul reproaches and rebukes those who show sorrow for those who have left this world. "I would not," he says, "like you to be ignorant, my dear brothers and sisters, about those who are sleeping, so that you feel sorrow like those who have no hope. If we believe that Jesus died and rose again, then God will bring those who are asleep in Jesus with him."

These who show sorrow at the departure of their friends reveal their own lack of hope. But we who live

111

by hope and believe in God, and are convinced that Christ suffered for us and that he rose again, who remain with Christ, and find our resurrection by him and in him, why should we either show reluctance when we ourselves have to depart or lament and grieve for others who depart as though they were dying forever? Christ himself, our Lord and God, tells us: "I am the resurrection and the life, he that believes in me, though he should die, shall live, and whoever lives and believes in me shall never die."

If we believe in Christ, let us put faith in his words and promises. Since we shall not die once and for all, let us pass into Christ in joy and confidence since we shall live and reign with him for ever.

(20-21)

Glory to Come

By dying here and now, we are transferred by that death to immortality, since we cannot approach eternal life without first leaving this life. Nor is this a departure but rather a transition, since we cross from the journey of this life to eternity. Who would not wish to arrive there as soon as possible? Who does not long to be transformed and made anew in the likeness of Christ, and to gain an early admittance to the dignity of heavenly grace?

Paul the apostle says: "Our true home is in heaven, from where we shall await Jesus Christ who will transform our mortal body, so that it is like the body of his glory." Christ the Lord has promised that we shall be in that state when he asks the Father that we may be with him and live with him in the place of eternity and be joyful in the realms of heaven: "Father, I wish that those who you have given to me should be with me and that they should see the glory which you gave me before the world began." They who are going to the seat of Christ, to the brightness of the heavenly kingdoms, ought not to weep and lament, but rather, according to the promise of the Lord, according to their belief in the truth, they should be joyful in their departure and change of state.

(22)

113

Freedom from the World

John in his epistle cries out and warns us that we should not become enamored of this world, while we indulge in desires of the flesh. "Do not," he says, "love this world nor the things in this world; if anyone loves the world then the love of the Father is not in him. For everything that is in the world, the lust of the flesh, the lust of the eyes, and the pride of life, is not of the Father, but of the lust of the world. And the world will pass away and the lust with it, but he who does the will of God shall last for ever, just as God shall last for ever." And so, my dear brothers and sisters, let us in the fullness of our spirit, with unshakable faith and steadfast courage, be ready to carry out the whole of God's will. Let us shut out our fear of death, and concentrate on the immortality which is to come. Let us live out our beliefs by not lamenting the departure of those we love and, when our own time comes, by going freely and without reluctance to the God who calls us.

(24)

Exiles Returning Home

We ought to consider, my dear brothers and sisters, and keep at the center of our thoughts the fact that we have renounced this world, and that we remain in this world as if we were just guests or strangers passing through. Let us embrace the day on which each one of us is assigned our final home, when, after we have finally been torn from this world and freed from its snares, we will enter paradise and the kingdom. Who travels abroad and does not want to return to their home as soon as they can? If someone is returning home to those they love, do they not long with all their heart for a fair wind so that they may embrace their friends the sooner? We can think of paradise as being like our native land where patriarchs will be our parents, so why should we not run in haste to see our country and to greet our parents? It is a large and loving community that is waiting for us there: parents, brothers, children, a great and varied gathering who long for us and who, safe in their own immortality, still feel anxiety for our salvation.

What gladness there shall be both for them and for us, when we enter their presence and their embrace! How sweet are the heavenly realms where death can never terrify us, and life can never end! What perfect and perpetual bliss! There we shall find the glorious company of the apostles; there the assembly of prophets exulting; there the great multitude of martyrs, crowned after their victory over strife and passion; there the virgins triumphant, who by their strength of will have overcome the desires of flesh and blood; there men and women of compassion, now themselves receiving com-

115

passion, who fulfilled the works of righteousness by giving food and sustenance to the poor, and who in obedience to the instructions of the Lord translated the inheritance of earth into the treasuries of heaven.

Let us hasten to these, my dear brothers and sisters, with eager longing. Let us desire to be quickly among them and seek to join Christ as soon as we are able. May God behold this thought of ours. May Christ take note of our intention and faith, and may he distribute the abundant rewards of his love all the more, the more that we desire them.

(26)

Selected Letters

Letter to the Confessors

Each one of you has been present to our affections, dear brothers and sisters, in the person of Celerinus, who is the companion of your faith and courage and the soldier of God in glorious battles. It is you whom we have seen in his arrival and, when he spoke so often and so sweetly of your love for me, it is your voice that I have heard. Great indeed is my joy when I receive messages of such things through such a messenger. Somehow we are present with you there in prison, and it seems to us that, being so close to you in our heart, we share the honor that the divine goodness grants you. Your glory becomes our glory by the love that unites us; this bond of love does not allow the spirits of those who love one another to be driven apart. We are both behind bars—you through your witness and myself through my affection for you. Mindful of you by day and by night, we ask God, both when we are praying with others during the eucharist and when we are praying alone, to grant you honor and the crown of victory.

But we are too poor to make you an adequate return. You give us far more when you remember us in your prayers, you whose hope is now only for heavenly things and who think only of things divine. You rise to a glory which is all the higher the longer your passion is delayed, since your glory is not diminished by the passage of time, but only increased.

A first and sole act of witness makes us blessed. But you, you repeat your witness every time that they offer to release you from prison, the prison which you your-selves have taken prisoner by your faith and your courage. Your praise is as great as the number of days you spend there, and the more the months pass, the greater is your increase in merit. They only conquer once who are executed immediately. But those whose sufferings endure, and who wrestle with pain without being conquered by it, are every day crowned anew.

II

There are now magistrates, consuls and proconsuls who glory in the insignia of their annual office. But in you the heavenly glory has shone forth for a whole year, and now the full cycle of the long and victorious year has turned. The rising sun filled the world with light as did the noon in its changing course, but in prison he who made the sun and the moon was your greater light. In your hearts and minds the radiance of Christ shone brightly, spreading its brilliant and eternal light through that place of pain, which is so grim and fearful for others.

The winter has progressed through the cycle of the months, while you in your prison have exchanged the season of winter for the winter of persecution. After winter spring has come, decked with roses and crowned with flowers. But your roses and flowers come from the gardens of paradise, and your heads are crowned with garlands from heaven.

And the summer too is coming, which is rich with harvest, when the threshing floor will be piled high with its fruits. But you who have sown the seeds of glory will reap a harvest of glory. As you lie on the threshing floor of God, you will see the chaff being burned by an inextinguishable fire. Yet you yourselves, like grains of corn winnowed from precious wheat, shall be preserved after the time of trial and shall find a granary in your prison to receive you.

Nor is autumn lacking in its own tasks for the spiritual season. The grapes which are gathered outdoors and which are to fill the goblets of wine are crushed in the press. So you too, like clusters of grapes from the Lord's vineyard, ripe and rich, are now crushed by the violence of the world's persecution in the prison which is like a press weighing upon you. Filled with the courage to endure your passion, you pour out your blood like a wine, willingly draining the martyr's cup.

This is how the year passes for the servants of God. Thus the cycle of the seasons is celebrated with spiritual merits and heavenly rewards.

III

Happy indeed are those of you who, having walked the path of glory and having finished the journey of courage and faith, have now departed from this world and have gone to receive the embrace and kiss of the Lord, who rejoices with you. But your glory is not less who, strong in battle and ready to follow your glorious companions, fight long and, remaining firm in immovable and unshakable faith, display your virtues with each new day to God. The longer your struggle, the more splendid your crown. There is a single contest for glory, though it is made up of many trials. You conquer hunger, you spurn thirst, and with your vigorous strength you overcome the filth of prison and the horror of that place of pain. There suffering is tamed, torment is destroyed, and death is not so much feared as desired. For it is overcome with the reward of immortality, so that they who conquer are granted eternal life. What a soul there is in you at the present moment! What a strong and noble heart is shown as you meditate upon such great things and as you think only of the precepts of God and the rewards of Christ! In your prison there is only the will of God, and although you are still in the body, the life which you live is not that of this world but of the next.

IV

It only remains for me, dearest brothers and sisters, to ask you now to remember me, to bear me in your minds and hearts in the midst of your great and godly thoughts and to make a place for me in your prayers and supplications. At this time your voice, which has been made glorious by the purification of witness and laudable by its perpetual notes of praise, reaches God's hearing. It passes beyond the world it has conquered and into heaven which stands open to it and obtains from the goodness of God everything it seeks.

For what do you ask of God's goodness that you do not deserve to receive? You who have kept so well the commandments of the Lord, who have kept the evangelical discipline with the vigor of a sincere faith and who by the uncorrupted honor of your virtue have stood firmly side by side with the precepts of the Lord and with his apostles. You have strengthened the wavering faith of many by the truth of your martyrdom. You are true witnesses to the gospel and true martyrs of Christ, who are supported by his roots and rest firmly upon the rock, and who have joined discipline with courage and led others to the fear of God. Your martyrdoms have become an example for all.

I hope that you, who are my strongest and most blessed brothers and sisters, will always conduct yourselves well and will always keep me in your memory.

Letter on the Eucharist

Since neither the apostle himself, nor an angel from heaven can announce or teach anything contrary to what Christ once taught and his apostles made known, I am eager to know what is the source of the new usage by which, in certain places, only water is offered in the Lord's cup. This is contrary to the evangelical and apostolic discipline, for water alone cannot represent the blood of Christ.

The Holy Spirit speaks of its significance too in the psalms when it is said of the cup of our Lord: "Your cup which inebriates is altogether excellent." A cup which inebriates certainly contains a mixture of wine. Water cannot make anyone drunk.

The cup of the Lord causes drunkenness, as Noah in Genesis becomes drunk when he drinks wine. But because the drunkenness of the Lord's cup and blood is not like the drunkenness that comes from the wine of the world, when the Holy Spirit says "Your cup which inebriates," he adds, "is altogether excellent." For the Lord's cup inebriates in such a way that it makes us sober. It restores our minds to spiritual wisdom, so that all turn from the taste of the world to the understanding of God. And just as the mind is loosened and the soul relaxed by worldly wine and all sadness is banished, in the same way when we drink from the blood and saving cup of our Lord, the old nature's memory is banished. It forgets its former worldly life and the sad and heavy breast, which was previously weighed down with the burden of sin. It is set free by the joy of divine mercy. But the Lord's cup, of course, cannot produce this joyful effect on those who drink from it in the Lord's Church unless a person holds fast to the truth.

II

Since Christ bore us, and bore our sins, we see that the water signifies the people, while the wine is the blood of Christ. Therefore when the water and the wine are mixed in the chalice, the people are united with Christ, and the great number of the faithful are joined and united with the one in whom they believe.

And this intermingling of water and wine in the chalice of our Lord is indissoluble. Hence the Church, that is the people who are firmly and faithfully established in the Church and who persevere in the faith, cannot ever be separated from Christ by anything, but will remain attached to him by a love that unites both as one.

And in the consecration of the Lord's cup, water alone cannot be offered, any more than wine alone can. For if someone offers the wine alone, then the blood of Christ is present without us, and if the water is offered alone, then we are present without Christ. But when both are mixed and are united one with the other, then the spiritual and heavenly mystery is perfected.

Thus the cup of our Lord is truly not water alone nor wine alone, without a mixture of the two. Just as the body of Christ cannot be either flour alone nor water alone without the two having been mixed together and unified in order to make up the bread.

Here too we find an image of the unity of our people. Just as many grains, which have been ground and mixed together, make up a single loaf, so in Christ, who is the bread of heaven, we know that we are one body in which our diversity is united and made one.

124

Cyprian's Final Letter

When I learned, dearest brothers and sisters, that police agents had been sent to bring me to Utique, and some very close friends advised me to withdraw for a while from my garden, I agreed to the plan; for it was well-founded. It is fitting in fact that a bishop should make his witness in that city in which he is the head of the Church, so that his confession of faith shall reflect on all the people there. Whatever a bishop says at the moment of his martyrdom, he says under the inspiration of God and on behalf of all. Otherwise something of the honor of our Church, which is so glorious, will be lost if I, the bishop of another Church, were to receive the sentence of martyrdom there and should go from there to meet the Lord.

It is in your midst that I wish to confess the Lord for myself and for all our sakes, and to suffer. It is from your midst that I wish to go to meet him. This is my duty, and I beg for it with all my prayers, desiring it greatly. And so here, in a hidden retreat, we are waiting for the return of the Proconsul to Carthage. We will hear from him what the rulers have ordered regarding the Christians, the laity and the bishops. And we will say what the Lord wants to be said in that moment.

As for you, dear brothers and sisters, remain calm, conforming to the evangelical discipline which you have always received from me, and to the teachings which you have so often learned from me. None of you should stir up the others or offer yourselves to the pagans. It is when we have been arrested and handed over to the magistrates that we should speak, for then the Lord

125

himself will speak in us, who demands from us not so much a profession of our faith as a martyr's confession of it.

As for what it would be fitting to do until the Proconsul sentences me to confess the name of God, we will decide that at the proper time, following the inspiration of the Lord.

I pray that the Lord Jesus will keep you secure in his Church, and that he will deign to preserve you there.

Short Bibliography

Texts and Translations (used for this anthology):

Bayard, L. *St. Cyprien: Correspondence*. Paris, 1925.

Mareschini, C. and Simonetti, M. *Sanctus Cyprianus Episcopus* (Corpus Christianorum Series Latina 3A). Turnhout, 1976.

Translations:

Wallis, R. E. in *Ante-Nicene Christian Library*. 2 vols. 1868-69.

Studies:

Benson, E. W. *Cyprian: His Life, His Times, His Work*. London, 1897.

Bettenson, Henry. *The Early Christian Fathers*, 263-73. London, 1956.

Quasten, Johannes. *Patrology*. Vol. 2, 340-83. Utrecht-Antwerp, 1953.